SOMERSET HOUSE

Splendour and Order

JOHN NEWMAN

PHOTOGRAPHS BY ANGELO HORNAK

© Scala Books 1990
Text © John Newman 1990

First published 1990
by Scala Publications Ltd
3 Greek Street
London W1V 6NX

All rights reserved

ISBN 1 870248 60 0

Designed by Roger Davies
Edited by Paul Holberton
Produced by Scala Publications
Filmset by August Filmsetting,
St Helens, England
Printed and bound by Graphicom,
Vicenza, Italy

Front cover View across the courtyard to the statue of George III and the dome over the centre of the river range.

Back cover Decorative railings from the Strand front.

Frontispiece Somerset House: the Strand façade, flanked by the houses which confined it to a frontage of only 135 ft [40.5 m].

Contents page Jean-Louis Desprez: *Idealised view of Somerset House, St Paul's Cathedral and Blackfriars Bridge* (Yale Centre for British Art, Paul Mellon collection). Compare page 40

Contents

The Commission

Ever since the destruction of Whitehall Palace by fire in 1698 there had been a recurrent ambition to build a great new classical palace in London. Inigo Jones's elaborate concept of a palace for Charles I published in 1727 fuelled public enthusiasm, but neither of the first two Georges showed the slightest interest in erecting a metropolitan seat of power. More realistic was the notion to rebuild the medieval Palace of Westminster, the seat of Parliament, leading William Kent in the 1730s to prepare a series of designs in the most grandiloquent Palladian style of the day. In 1739 such a scheme was about to receive Treasury approval, but Sir Robert Walpole's administration fell. So it was left to two government buildings in Whitehall to set new standards of public architecture in mid-Georgian London. In 1733–35 a new Treasury building was erected facing Horse Guards Parade. Though only a fragment of William Kent's full scheme, it established rusticated Portland stonework as the proper garb for such buildings. Fifteen years later the Horse Guards Building was rebuilt in similar style on the basis of a design by Kent, forming in effect a new War Office. Britain being a maritime power, there was perhaps only one further government department which would justify a similar treatment, the Navy Office.

The present Somerset House was built primarily to provide modern accommodation for the Navy Office. Ideas for rehousing the office in a more convenient situation were in the air by the 1760s. But at this stage nothing like the present building was envisaged, just a 'plain building' for £30,000, less than half the cost of the Horse Guards.

There were other complicating factors. Numerous small government offices, some of them vital producers of tax revenue, were scattered throughout London. In 1768 the Excise Office, one of the most important, gained new premises in Old Broad Street. An alternative, more westerly, site considered for this had been Ely House, Holborn, and in 1771 the Bishop of Ely again offered to sell it to the Crown for a public use. This prompted the Treasury to envisage bringing the remaining revenue offices together into a single building and in 1772 Ely House was acquired. But no preparations were made to build on the site,

and two years later attention turned instead to the Thames-side, in order presumably to provide more conveniently for the river transport of goods. In 1773–74 a plan was prepared for new offices on the site of the Savoy Palace, and in May 1774 the embankment was discussed of the foreshore in front of it and of its immediate neighbour to the east, Somerset House.

Somerset House, built in the mid-sixteenth century by Edward Seymour, Duke of Somerset, regent for Edward VI, had at his death become Crown property. From the time of James I it had regularly served as the Queen's dower house, an arrangement which George III had renewed by an Act of 1761. Over the years the Tudor palace had been extended and modernised, in particular by the river gallery range of 1661–64 believed to represent a design by Inigo Jones, and by the adjacent façade by William Kent of 1743. Queen Charlotte, however, did not use the palace and by the early 1770s it was becoming dilapidated. Its fate was sealed quite suddenly in 1774: on 6 May the Board of Works reported that large parts of the palace were collapsing or had already collapsed, and eleven days later the King agreed to its total demolition so that public buildings could be erected on the site. In exchange Buckingham House was to become the Queen's dower house, and these arrangements were enshrined in an Act passed in May 1775.

Here then was the site for the new public offices. But who was to be architect for this extensive commission? The obvious, unimaginative choice was William Robinson, the Secretary to the Board of Works. No one had more relevant experience. Throughout the 1750s he had been joint supervising architect for the Horse Guards, and his Excise Office was a brand new if not particularly impressive demonstration of his capabilities in this direction. The Treasury had employed him to survey Ely House and to make the plans for the Savoy site. Within the Office of Works he also happened to be Clerk at Somerset House. By April 1775 Robinson had prepared plans for two parallel ranges, one mainly devoted to the Navy Office, the other for the revenue offices together with offices for the Duchies of

4

Cornwall and Lancaster and apartments for the Royal Academy. His estimate for these, and for embanking the Thames, amounted to £135,700.

What would have been the architectural character of Robinson's Somerset House can only be guessed; however, the issue was discussed in Parliament at the end of the month, when, as Lord North informed the King, 'there was a little dispute . . . about the expence of building the design'd Offices, Mr Burke pressing for Splendor, & Mr Townshend recommending economy'. Robinson was accordingly instructed to design a building that would be 'an ornament to the Metropolis and a monument of the taste and elegance of His Majesty's Reign'. In the succeeding few months no further progress is recorded, and in October Robinson suddenly died. Within the month Sir William Chambers was appointed architect in his stead, at the King's express desire, so it was reported.

Fate thus finally presented to Chambers the great commission for which his career had been a preparation, and which, as Comptroller in the Office of Works and thus Robinson's superior, he should by rights have received at the outset. The eighteen months from the spring of 1774 to the autumn of 1775 were an unsettled time for him. Two major private jobs were coming to an end, Gower House in Whitehall and Melbourne House, Piccadilly, while the important commission to rebuild his own parish church of St Marylebone fell through in 1774; so he had nothing significant on hand except the cantankerous Lord Dorchester's 'vast, ugly Gothick house', Milton Abbey, Dorset. Worse still, the King, who had been Chambers's pupil in his youth and to whom the *Treatise on Civil Architecture* (1759) had been gratefully dedicated, was still unable after thirteen years of dithering to decide whether to commission from him a new palace at Richmond. In August 1775 Chambers was still writing ruefully, 'My Model for Richmond palace is finished but when the building begins is not yet determined'. It never began. Yet it was at this time that Chambers travelled abroad once again. He visited Paris for several weeks during May and June 1774, meeting the French artists he had got to know in Rome twenty years earlier, many of them now at the peak of their careers, the painters Doyen, Greuze and Hubert Robert, the sculptor Pajou, and among architects all the competitors for the current commission to build the new theatre of the Comédie Française, Moreau-Desproux, Peyre and de Wailly. But too much of his visit was not to be wasted in socialising, for, he insisted, he had come 'with a view to Observe and not to Eat'. He recorded in a series of beautiful watercolours the major new public works which had been springing up in Paris in the peaceful years after the end of the Seven Years War, Gabriel's Ecole Militaire and Place Louis Quinze (Place de la Concorde), J.D. Antoine's Hôtel des Monnaies (Mint) (see below)

Sir William Chambers: Hôtel des Monnaies, Paris, 1768–75 by J. D. Antoine, façade towards the river Seine (Royal Institute of British Architects)
This beautiful wash drawing is one of a group recording new buildings seen by Chambers in Paris in 1774. The building itself influenced the design of Somerset House in several respects.

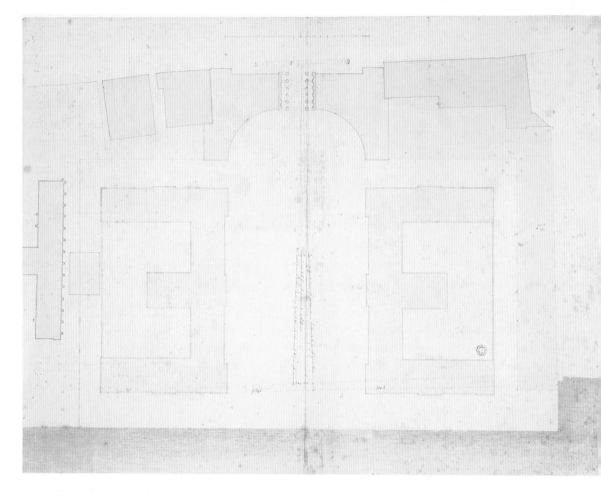

Sir William Chambers: Preliminary block plan for Somerset House (Sir John Soane's Museum)
Here the architect has experimented with a layout of three distinct blocks surrounding a courtyard open to the river, reminiscent of the broad lines of Wren's Greenwich Hospital. It is one of at least four quite different schemes which Chambers seems to have explored at a time when he had little prospect of gaining the commission to build Somerset House.

and Gondoin's Ecole de Chirurgie. Here was a source of inspiration and envy, for in England, as he bitterly remarked, architects 'have little or no encouragement'.

Did this visit bear any relation to Chambers's ambitions towards the new public offices? He reached Paris on 2 May 1774, four days before the submission of the damning report on Old Somerset House, but he must have known what the report would conclude. He himself later admitted that he had made several plans 'When the Business of Somerset House was first talked of'. This perhaps helps to explain the venom with which he attacked Robinson, 'a Clerk in our office, ill qualified', whereas 'the King has Six Architects in his Service ready and able to obey his Commands. Methinks it should be otherwise in the Reign of a Vertuoso Prince'. Also galling was the inclusion of the Royal Academy of Arts in the brief for the new building. Chambers, as the Academy's Treasurer, had in 1771 negotiated the accommodation of the fledgling institution in Old Somerset House, and now frustratingly it seemed he was to be debarred from designing its new premises.

What must be some of Chambers's 1774 plans survive in Sir John Soane's Museum. There are at least four different schemes, some abandoned at an early stage and all illustrating a fairly cavalier approach to the difficulties of the site. His attention was focussed primarily on grandiose columned vestibules and on staircases of impressive scale and form.

Nevertheless, when Chambers unexpectedly received the commission at the end of October 1775, it took him, aided by these preliminary trials, only three months to elaborate his final design.

The site was a difficult one and Chambers faced up to the challenge of exploiting it to the full. The frontage to the Strand was a mere 135 ft [41 m]. Behind that the palace, its gardens and stables extended over an area 400 ft [122 m] deep and nearly 700 ft [213 m] wide between Duchy Lane to the west and Strand Lane to the east. Furthermore there was a drop of nearly 40 ft [12 m] across the site from the Strand to the river's edge. From his earliest project Chambers was determined to replace the Strand-facing Tudor block with an entrance range centred on an elaborate columned vestibule, through which access would open to one or more spacious court-yards. He toyed with the idea of an oval courtyard surrounded by streets on three sides, and with a double courtyard plan that had a circular court at the front and a rectangular one towards the river beyond, and he tried out an arrangement of three monumental ranges forming a courtyard open towards the river (see opposite). In the former two he was dependant on Inigo Jones's designs for Whitehall Palace, and in the last on Wren's Greenwich Hospital. His final solution related more naturally to the site than any of these. A single courtyard, about 200 ft [61 m] wide and 300 ft [91 m] deep is flanked by side streets and terraces of houses, linked together towards the river to form a façade 500 ft [152 m] long standing above a lofty river-side terrace which takes up virtually the full drop in the ground.

All Chambers's thinking ran along the lines of splendour. Burke's arguments in its favour had been made in April 1775 while the commission was still held by Robinson. Chambers recognised the impor-tance of Burke's intervention, and on one occasion even told him that Somerset House was 'a Child of your own'. But first of all, once he had received the commission, Chambers had to face the practical problem of allocating the available space to the vari-ous bodies (see page 8). The learned societies he placed in the pre-eminent position, in the Strand block. The vaults extending vastly under the north-ern part of the courtyard were intended as a repository for the public records. The government offices varied considerably in size, nor did they remain static during the long building period, so some of Chambers's dispositions had to be modified when the time came, in the late 1780s onwards, for the building to be occupied. Each office, regardless of size, was allocated a vertical slice of accommodation, extending through all six storeys – cellar, basement, ground, principal, attic and garret. Besides the working office space, housing was needed for caretakers and for the Secret-aries and Receivers who ran the offices. The Com-missioners of the Navy and Victualling offices were to occupy the nine houses in the terrace west of the courtyard (see page 9), and at the river end of this the Treasurer of the Navy was allotted an elegant man-sion, with coach houses and stabling for ten horses in the vaults under the river terrace.

The Navy Office was sited in the west half of the principal, river-ward range of the courtyard, with the related Sick and Hurt, Navy Pay and Victualling Offices in the west range, the Stamp Office in the east half of the river range, and in the east range other tax offices flanking the Duchy of Cornwall office. The west wing of the Strand block towards the courtyard was at first allocated to the Treasury Remembrancer, but in 1780 was fitted up for the Office of Hawkers and Pedlars; the east wing was fitted as the Hackney Coach Office, but was soon taken over by the Exchequer Office.

Money for the new building came direct from the Treasury. There had been an initial cost of £100,000, granted to the King to purchase Buck-ingham House, which put the site of Somerset House into the Treasury's hands. The building costs them-selves could be partially offset by the eventual sale of the sites of the various offices which were to be rehoused and by savings in rent payments. It was calculated that £99,550 would be realised in these ways and by leasing out part of the site of the old palace not required for building, and this looked quite a healthy state of affairs so long as Robinson's estimate of £135,700 was on the table. Chambers supplied no initial estimate, and at the end of 1779, after four years' work, when the shell of the Strand block was complete but nothing much else had risen above ground, £88,000 had already been spent. In extenuation Chambers claimed that the building was 'of a very uncommon Kind, unusually extensive,

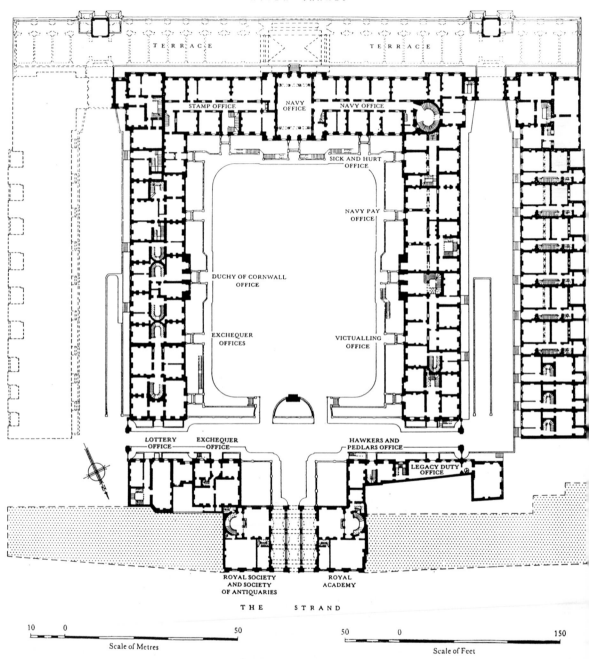

RIVER THAMES

TERRACE   TERRACE

STAMP OFFICE   NAVY OFFICE   NAVY OFFICE

SICK AND HURT OFFICE

NAVY PAY OFFICE

DUCHY OF CORNWALL OFFICE

EXCHEQUER OFFICES   VICTUALLING OFFICE

LOTTERY OFFICE   EXCHEQUER OFFICE   HAWKERS AND PEDLARS OFFICE

LEGACY DUTY OFFICE

ROYAL SOCIETY AND SOCIETY OF ANTIQUARIES   ROYAL ACADEMY

THE STRAND

10   0   50   50   0   150

Scale of Metres   Scale of Feet

Somerset House: General plan at ground-floor level (copyright Her Majesty's Stationery Office)
The embankment terrace is shown dotted since it stands below ground level; the dotted block to the east, however, is Chambers's unexecuted terrace of houses later replaced by King's College. The building in general is shown as it was when declared complete in 1801, with the addition of the Legacy Duty Office, built 1817–22.

intricately complicated and attended with many and great Difficulties in the Execution'. For this reason it was still impossible to give an estimate though he made the calculation, or rather guess, that a further six and a half years would suffice to execute the whole design at a total cost of £250,000. In both respects this proved a hopeless underestimate. The building was not declared complete until 1801, five years after the death of the architect, when the total expenditure came to £462,323. Yet even then a quarter of Chambers's design remained unbuilt. Eventually in 1831–35 the eastern third of the river front was completed to the original design as part of King's College, which had been begun by Sir Robert Smirke in 1829 with a new block of his own design in place of Chambers's proposed eastern terrace.

Somerset House: View to the western 'Palladian bridge'
This high-level shot shows on the right the terraced houses of the Navy Commissioners with the house of the Treasurer of the Navy in the far right corner. The relationship of the arched bridge to the transparent pedimented colonnade is clearly seen. Beyond is the river terrace.

The Craftsmen and the Architect

Among the notes he made in 1771 for lectures he intended to give to the Royal Academy (but which were never read), Chambers translated an observation made by François Blondel in his *Cours d'Architecture* as follows: 'There are three things to be observed in a fine building, the Workmanship, the Splendour, and the Composition; the honour of the first of these is due to the Workman, of the second to the Proprietor, and of the third to the Architect.' The Treasury, in the role of 'Proprietor' or client, by allowing the money to continue to flow over a period of twenty-five years secured the splendour of Somerset House. To Chambers himself, of course, was due the 'Composition'. But the workmen also deserve recognition. The mid-Georgian period set new standards of craftsmanship in the building trades, partly because Chambers and other leading architects insisted on unprecedented precision of execution.

Somerset House was constructed by teams of bricklayers, masons, carpenters and slaters, fitted up by teams of plumbers, glaziers, joiners and smiths, and finished by teams of carvers, plasterers and painters. Most of the master craftsmen who headed the teams had already worked for Chambers. This was true of Edward Gray and John Groves, who shared the bricklaying contracts with Henry and Richard Holland (of Holland & Co., one of the biggest operators of the day). They built the carcasses of the walls, but their craftsmanship can be seen best in the subterranean vaults constructed of greystock with yellow cut-and-rubbed 'malms' forming the groins (see below). Two teams of masons, those of

Somerset House: Vaults
Intended for storage of the National Records, the vaults extend southwards under the courtyard for the full width of the Strand block and its wings as far as the balustraded area. There is evidence that the brickwork, of purplish 'greystocks' and yellow cut-and-rubbed 'malms', was meant originally to be exposed as it is now.

Somerset House: Vestibule, looking west
This is the 'ceremonial' doorway on the Royal Academy side surmounted by Joseph Wilton's bust of Michelangelo, but not the real entrance, which is in the adjacent bay to the left. Here the beautiful quality of the Portland stone masonry (John Devall master mason) can be well appreciated.

John Devall and John Gilliam, worked side by side throughout the building period cutting and setting the Portland stone facings which have worn so well that the precision and variety of their tooling can still be enjoyed (see opposite). The carpentry, by contrast, is almost all concealed, the trusses of oak, framing of fir and boarding of deal; the master carpenters were James Filewood, and from 1779 Samuel Wyatt, the most innovative carpenter of the day as well as a distinguished architect. John Westcott, whose men laid Westmoreland slates on the roofs, Messrs. Devall & Holroyd, the principal plumbers, and Richard and John Cobbett, the glaziers, had all worked for the architect before. William Palmer, the smith, died in 1779, and his executors supplied the iron gates and balustrades which embellish the Strand block (see right). A variety of joiners were employed, George Neale, William Clarke, James Arrow, and the Master Joiner in the Office of Works, William Greenell. The decorative plasterwork in the Strand block (see right) was in the hands of Thomas Clark, the Master Plasterer, and Thomas Collins, who was both an outstandingly skilful plasterer and one of Chambers's closest associates and partner with him in property development. Among the carvers Joseph Wilton, another longtime acquaintance and colleague of Chambers, contracted for the bulk of the chimneypieces, though Richard Hayward later supplied a good many. The carvers who specialized in putting the finishing touches to such details as stone capitals and timber door-cases were Richard Lawrence and Sefferin Alken, the latter a craftsman whose skill the architect particularly admired.

Figure sculptors had a major role to play in the decoration of Somerset House, and here too Wilton was the most widely employed. A list of the sculptors, whom Chambers carefully selected, reads like a roll-call of the sculptor members of the Royal Academy: John Bacon, Agostino Carlini, Joseph Nollekens, Joseph Wilton, together with a young Italian protégé of the architect, Giuseppe Ceracchi. The same is true of the painters whose works adorned the ceilings of the apartments of the learned societies in the Strand block, G.B. Cipriani, Benjamin West, Angelica Kauffmann, J.F. Rigaud and even the President himself, Sir Joshua Reynolds. Charles Catton contributed decorative paintings and headed

Somerset House: Ironwork panel in front of the Strand façade
This robust but unconventional design is repeated eight times in the railings which protect passers-by from falling into the areas that light the basements under the Strand block.

Sir William Chambers: Preliminary designs for plasterwork (Sir John Soane's Museum)
The main drawing is for the guilloche bands which run round the stairwells in the Strand block at two levels. The lyre motif was included in the executed plasterwork, but the vase motif was replaced by a lion's head in a rosette. The lower sketch is for the central Ionic heads of the coffered arches supporting the top landings.

Sir William Chambers: Part elevation of an early design for the river front (Victoria and Albert Museum)
This extremely interesting drawing differs in numerous ways from what was built, particularly in the Doric order of the portico; yet the small dome is already present.

one of the firms which painted walls and ceilings, William Evans heading the other.

Supervision fell to the architect's most trusted assistants, the clerks of works John Yenn and Robert Browne, together with Thomas Clark, superintendent of the works, assisted by a succession of talented young students of the Royal Academy Schools. In control of everyone was Sir William Chambers himself, for whom the wealth-producing activity of the craftsmen was as satisfying as the realisation of his own artistic concept, as he wrote in 1784: 'When ever I see, as I do very often, five or six hundred industrious fellows supporting themselves and their familys, many of them growing rich, under my command; I feel such a pleasure as no General ever felt in War, be the Victory what it might. My troops conquer their difficulties, & carry health and plenty to their habitations. His conquests are the purchase of blood, Rapine, murder, desolation; maimed bodies & distracted minds. His business is to destroy, mine is to create, his to ruin the World & Rob Mankind of every blessing, while mine is to enrich, to beautify it, and to supply its inhabitants with every comfort.'

About 800 drawings survive for Somerset House, from preliminary plans to highly finished presentation drawings (see above and right), including many which explore particular problems of construction or decoration. Not all of these, of course, are in Chambers's own hand; the majority must be by his assistants, but many could only have been drawn by the architect himself, and even more bear notes in his handwriting, so that taken as a whole the drawings

Sir William Chambers: Finished pen and wash elevation of the entrance doorway in the Strand block west wing (Sir John Soane's Museum)
This drawing, of exhibition quality, corresponds closely with what was built – but note the sex of the mask-head. The Treasury Remembrancer was replaced by the Hawkers and Pedlars Office.

Somerset House: Doorway to the east wing of the Strand block
This was the entrance to the Hackney Coach (later Exchequer) Office. On the keystone the horned male head of a 'tutelary spirit' was carved by Nollekens.

demonstrate Chambers's deep involvement with virtually every aspect of the design of the building. When he obtained the commission in 1775 he was fifty-two, and could have looked forward to another two decades of varied practice. Instead he recognised that Somerset House could be the great work to immortalize his name and for the next twenty years, until ill health forced his retirement, he devoted all his professional attention to it. Only one other commission tempted him, for monumental barracks on the adjacent Savoy site, for which he presented plans in 1777, 1782 and 1788, 'a complete set of designs', as he called them in 1795.

For Chambers Somerset House was not just a personal artistic statement, nor was it only a monumental expression of national pride, though it was both those things. It was also an opportunity to set out the principles of architectural design as he saw them. The didactic streak in him was strong. Early royal patronage had led to his appointment in 1757 as architectural tutor to the Prince of Wales, the future George III, and this in turn formed the foundation of his most important publication, *The Treatise on Civil Architecture* (1759), a theoretical work which at once established itself as the best organized and most authoritative publication in English on classical architecture. Throughout the busy years of his professional career he spent much thought on the revision of the book, leading to the enlarged third edition of 1791.

Chambers's natural architectural vocabulary was the Palladianism which he had imbibed in his youth: he found much to admire in Kent and Gibbs. However, his training in Paris at the academy of J.F. Blondel, followed by years of study and travel in Italy, gave him a breadth of reference which ranged from the Italian Renaissance of Bramante, Raphael and Peruzzi through the Baroque of Bernini and Cortona to include an interest in modern French decoration, both the *rocaille* fantasies of Meissonier and Oppenord and the *'gout grec'* of Legeay and Petitot. His visit to Paris in 1774 brought his knowledge of French architecture up to date. But of some current trends in architectural design in both France and England he did not approve. Both the archaeological discoveries of the 1750s which led to a positive reassessment of ancient Greek architecture and the reductive rationalism of the Abbé Laugier's *Essai sur l'architecture* (1753) were in his view stultifying and a threat to the rich tradition of the past 250 years which he had assimilated. Nor was he enamoured of the quest for 'novelty' trumpeted by his great rival Robert Adam. Adam's architectural (if not financial) success in his riverside Adelphi development a few hundred yards upstream together with the commencement in 1774 of his first major public building, The Register House in Edinburgh, must have given an edge to Chambers's determination to demonstrate his architectural beliefs in durable stone.

The Exterior

Somerset House is fundamentally Palladian, in that it can be seen to form a series of variations on a theme by Inigo Jones. It also deploys the classical orders, Doric, Ionic, Composite and Corinthian (in the sequence which Chambers had illustrated in his *Treatise* (see right)), and associates features such as window-surrounds, doorways and cornice mouldings with one or other of these orders so that they reinforce order and hierarchy at every point. This applies as much to the interior of the building as to the exterior. However, symbolic decoration and a variety of spatial effects, some of them very dramatic, enrich this basic syntax.

Chambers's theme is stated on the Strand front, a rusticated arcaded ground storey with above it a *piano nobile* and a square-windowed mezzanine linked together by a Corinthian order of half columns (see page 16). This characteristic Palladian composition, stemming back ultimately to Bramante, is here inescapably reminiscent of the Jonesian river gallery of Old Somerset House (see page 18). This, however, was only five bays wide, set on five open arches, and required no central emphasis. Chambers's 135 ft [41 m] front by contrast had to provide an entrance to which the architecture must draw attention. So he formed a façade of nine bays, of which only the central three have open arches, and above these he crowned the skyline with an attic in a way suggested to him by two modern Continental buildings which he admired, Salvi's Fontana di Trevi in Rome and Antoine's Parisian Mint. The attic has the incidental function of hiding the great windows of the Exhibition Room, which are incompatible with the architectural theme. Within the side arches of the ground floor Chambers placed Doric window aedicules, while those of the *piano nobile* are Ionic, and by making the main entablature Composite rather than Corinthian he managed to introduce the full gamut of the orders into the façade. An anonymous author of 1778, quoted in Baretti's *Guide* of 1781, and widely assumed to be Chambers himself, explained the intended effect of the Strand front: 'All that the Artist could do in so small a compass, and all that he seems to have attempted, was to produce an object, that should indicate something more considerable within,

and excite the Spectator's curiosity to a nearer examination of the whole, of which it made a part. His style in consequence is bold, simple, and regular. It is an attempt to unite the chastity and order of the Venetian Masters with the majestick grandeur of the Roman. The parts are few, large, and distinct. The transitions sudden, and strongly marked. No breaks in the general course of the Plan, and little movement in the outline of the Elevation; whence

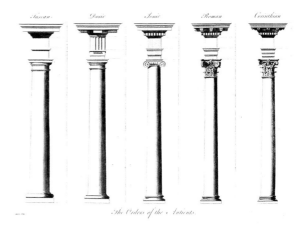

The Orders of the Antients

Sir William Chambers: Engraving of the five orders, from the *Treatise on Civil Architecture*
This plate provides a convenient means of comparing the proportions and details of the five orders with one another. Note that Chambers places the Composite between the Ionic and the Corinthian, not, like most theorists, at the end of the series.

Somerset House: Strand front (*following page*)
Here Chambers establishes the Palladian theme of the whole building. The front faces north-west, so it is rarely seen sunlit. However this photograph, taken on a summer evening, brings out the qualities which the architect particularly sought: 'The parts are few, large, and distinct. The transitions sudden and strongly marked ... whence the whole structure has acquired an air of consequence.'

Antonio Canaletto: *Old Somerset House seen from the Thames* (private collection) (*pages 18–19*)
This view, painted about 1750, shows prominently in the centre of the south front of the old palace the arcaded river gallery built in 1661–64 and believed in the eighteenth century to have been designed by Inigo Jones. Chambers used it as the source for the design of his Strand façade.

15

the whole Structure has acquired an air of conse-quence, to which its dimensions do not intitle it.'

After this the colonnaded vestibule is a shock and a delight, one of the most imaginatively managed spaces in the whole building (see opposite). The triple vault one has been prepared for, but not the coupling of the Doric columns nor the crisp, uncon-ventional Doric detailing, the first evidence that there is more to Chambers than the scrupulous pedagogue. Baretti suggests that 'The general idea of this Vesti-bule seems taken from that of the great Farnese-palace at Rome, designed by Antonio Sangallo; yet so altered in its forms, proportions, and decorations, that scarce any resemblance to the Original remains'. He refrains from mentioning three splendid vestibules, all with coupled columns, which the architect had recently seen in Paris, at the Mint, at the Louvre (particularly similar in its vaulting), and at the Ecole Militaire by Gabriel, probably the source for much of Chambers's detailing.

In the courtyard beyond, the Jonesian theme is re-established. On the back of the Strand block it is simply restated, with pilasters instead of half columns and an arcade only in the three central entry bays. To left and right wings come forward, and here the first variation is played, for above the rusticated ground storey the rustication goes right up until it reaches the main entablature, setting off the Corinthian pilasters, which swell out into half columns on the front faces of the wings (see page 22). Since the learned societies were confined to the Strand block itself but govern-ment offices occupied the wings, this overall rus-tication establishes the architectural connection between the new offices and the earlier Treasury and Horse Guards, both rusticated overall. The rus-tication also goes down below ground level, where arcaded light wells left and right of the roadway accommodate basement water tanks.

The three main ranges of the courtyard (see pages 24–25) present a heavily rusticated appearance,

relieved by smooth walling and pedimented windows in the centre of the river-ward range and at the ends of the side ranges. The ranges stand at a level a few feet lower than the Strand block, and since they were to be entirely occupied by offices they clearly must be felt as subordinate to the block in which the learned societies were installed. On the other hand the view through the vestibule and across the courtyard had to lead to a visual climax. This Chambers pro-vided by the small dome over the centre of the river range. The dome rests on a lightweight drum con-structed not of stone but of timber and is in a curi-ously ambiguous relation to the architecture below, rising behind a sculptured pediment which itself rests on a timber attic visually unconnected with the colonnaded centrepiece. The centrepiece itself con-sists of four Composite columns set between square pilasters over which the entablature and crowning balustrade break forward. This feature is repeated as the centrepiece of each side range. The appearance here for the first time of columns in the round gives a further sense of architectural development. Yet the progression from Corinthian on the Strand block to Composite here is, in Chambers's scheme of the orders, a move downwards, so the subordination of the courtyard to the Strand block is reaffirmed.

The final architectural set piece of Somerset House had to be the river front (see page 25). This was designed to be more than $2\frac{1}{2}$ times the 210 ft [64 m] width of the courtyard, yet the same dome and identi-cal pediment and columned centrepiece had to pro-vide the central stress, a task for which they were manifestly insufficient.

In two other important ways, however, Chambers developed his architectural theme further on the river front. First he underpinned it with a massively rusti-cated arcade. Functionally this provided embank-ment with vaulted storage space behind and carried a promenade terrace, but visually it forms a mighty substructure to the whole composition. In the centre the arcade is interrupted by a yawning semicircular arch through which boats could slide in to the storage vaults. To east and west, aligned on the two streets which descended to the river on either side of the courtyard ranges, are two water-gates, based on another Jonesian model, the York House water-gate half-a-mile upstream.

Second, within the river front itself, Chambers introduced his Composite *piano nobile* order more powerfully than anywhere else, above the 'Palladian bridges' which align with the water-gates and span the side streets by means of daringly wide semicircular arches with elegant mouldings and sculpture. The colonnades which stand on them repeat the central motif of the façade but transform it since they are transparent and carry a pediment, thus creating the only temple-front compositions in the whole of Somerset House (see page 27). To frame and enhance the pedimented bridges further, there project three-bay flanking sections of the façade, enriched with pilasters and pedimented windows.

Today Chambers's monumental composition is undermined by the Victorian embankment which has buried the lowest courses of masonry, rendered the central arch useless and deprived the water-gates of their steps (see page 26). Even the bosky plane trees disguise the architect's intention, which was to make the river front appear as a long, low, white, palace delicately poised on the strong but shadowy arcading of the terrace. (Other important additions to the context of Somerset House are Waterloo Bridge (1811–17, rebuilt 1938) and the west-facing addition to Somerset House itself, the Inland Revenue Building built in 1856 by James Pennethorne in a pastiche of Chambers's design.)

This highly cerebral creation is enlivened by a variety of architectural detailing. Chambers took enormous pains over details, and rang changes on them throughout the building, so that for example the pedimented *piano nobile* windows, superficially the same throughout, are in fact of three different designs, one on the Strand block, another in the courtyard and a third on the river façade, subtleties which are normally appreciated only at a subliminal level.

The sculpture on the building is a different matter. It is symbolic and meant to be understood. The main

Somerset House: the Strand block and its wings seen from the courtyard
This view shows Chambers's architecture in all its concentration of richness. Here only he introduced a mezzanine over the ground storey, making the buildings seven storeys high (including two below ground and one hidden in the roof). The foreground balustrade marks the area from which the vaults for the National Records gained light.

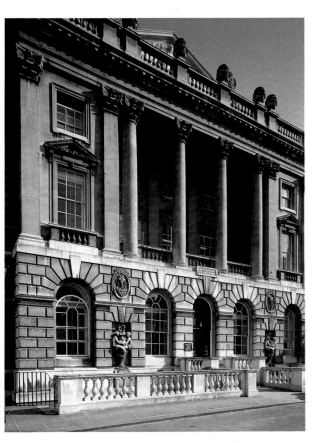

Somerset House: Courtyard looking northwest
(*far left, above*)
Rustication dominates the walls of the courtyard ranges. This view also shows how the Strand block stands higher than the courtyard ranges. Only when the cars have gone can the original effect of the courtyard be recaptured.

Somerset House: South range centrepiece
(*far left, below*)
A close-up view shows that the stone-work stops at balustrade level and that the attic, pediment and dome drum are all of painted timber. The relief, by Richard Rathbone, an otherwise unknown carver, represents a sea-borne nymph.

Somerset House: South range of the courtyard, central section (*left*)
This composition is a complex variation of the Jonesian theme stated on the Strand façade. The doorway, leading into the Seamen's Hall of the Navy Office, is flanked by Joseph Wilton's sculptural groups of tribute-bearing tritons.

Somerset House: River front seen from Waterloo Bridge (*below*)
When Somerset House was first built there was no bridge across the Thames at this point, but the distant view from the south bank was clearly important. The four bays to the left belong to Pennethorne's Inland Revenue building of the 1850s.

Somerset House: Arcaded embankment wall of the river terrace (*left, above*)
This view along the 500 ft [152.4 m] terrace shows in the foreground one of the two water-gates, which were consciously modelled by Chambers on the York House water-gate, then believed to be by Inigo Jones. Here the rustication has a rugged texture and here alone, at this lowest level, the order is Tuscan. Originally one could embark from steps below the water-gate.

Somerset House: the river terrace (*right*)
This was intended by Chambers to be one of the most important architectural experiences of the whole building, a promenade 500 ft [152.4 m] long accessible from the Seamen's Hall in the centre and from the water's edge up flights of steps within the water-gates.

Somerset House: Strand front keystone (*left, below*)
The keystones of the nine arches of the ground-floor arcade are carved with bearded heads representing Ocean and the rivers of England. This is Medway, with plaited beard to symbolize its placid character, a ship's prow (for Chatham Dockyard), fruit and hops (for the Garden of England). Joseph Wilton was the sculptor, to a design probably by Chambers.

themes are patriotic, celebrating the naval power and imperial ambitions of Great Britain, at a time when both were expanding greatly in spite of the contemporary setback of the American War of Independence (1774–83). On the Strand front the keystones of the arcade are carved with vividly differentiated bearded heads. The central one represents Ocean, and is flanked by eight English rivers, in order from the centre westwards, Thames, Humber, Mersey and Dee, and eastwards, Medway (see left below), Tweed, Tyne and Severn. Wilton carved all except Dee, Tyne and Severn, which are by Carlini. Above, at *piano nobile* level, the central three window pediments bear Wilton's garlanded medallion portraits of George III, Queen Charlotte and the Prince of Wales. Against the attic stand four colossal statues, the inner by Carlini, the outer by Ceracchi. These represent 'venerable Men in senatorial robes, with the cap of liberty on their heads. All of them have in one hand a Fasces composed of reeds firmly bound together, an emblem of Strength derived from unanimity, while the other hand of each Figure sustains respectively, the Scales, the Mirrour, the Sword, and the Bridle; Symbols of Justice, Prudence, Valour and Moderation; qualities by which Dominion can alone be maintained'. (Baretti, *Guide*.) Crowning the attic

is John Bacon's shield of arms of the British Empire, supported by the figures of Fame and the Genius of England.

The corresponding figures on the attic facing the courtyard are by Wilton and represent the four continents, three of them bearing cornucopias of tribute (see above), but America, second from the left, 'armed and breathing defiance', a surprising and encouraging acknowledgement of reality! Bacon's skyline group here consists of the British arms supported by tritons who hold nets full of fish. The keystones to the vestibule arches were carved by Nollekens with three identical female masks, which Baretti identifies as the 'Lares; or tutelar Deities of the Place'. Two more, male these ones, are over the doorways to the wings. Crowning the parapets of the wings are pairs of lead sphinxes, cast by John Cheere, flanking

Somerset House: the Strand block, attic towards the courtyard. The statues, executed by Joseph Wilton in 1778, represent the four continents, Europe, Asia, Africa and America. They bear cornucopias, 'loaded with tributary fruits and treasures', except America (second left), which is shown 'armed and breathing defiance'. The shield of arms of Great Britain above, with a fish-filled net suspended from it, was carved by John Bacon, and cost £367. 10s. 0d.

Roman altars which disguise chimney stacks.

The courtyard itself is dominated by a bronze statue of George III, standing toga-clad against an antique prow and holding a rudder, while Father Thames reclines below (see left). For this the sculptor, John Bacon, received the formidable sum of £2000 when it was erected in 1789. Flanking the central doorways of the courtyard ranges and in the centre of the river front are four pairs of urns overflowing with tribute which tritons struggle to support. Those in the south range, with their marine tackle, relate to the Navy Office, those in the west range, brimming with animal heads, indicate where the Victualling Office was located, and those in the east range show corn and fruit, for the Duchy of Cornwall's office. Wilton also executed these in 1787. Above are oval relief heads of appropriate deities, Bacchus, Ceres, Neptune etc. This part of the programme of sculpture seems to have been an afterthought and the urns project awkwardly from their shallow niches (see below). The courtyard skyline is less significant: in the pediment is Richard Rathbone's relief of a sea-borne nymph and flanking it are trophies of arms sculpted by Thomas Banks; otherwise there are only groups of draped Coadestone vases.

Within the Strand block the apartments of the learned societies have their own elaborate decoration. They are heralded in the vestibule by two busts by Wilton, on the Royal Academy's side Michelangelo, 'the first of artists', and opposite on the Royal Society's side Sir Isaac Newton, 'the first of philosophers'.

Somerset House: View looking south across the courtyard
In the foreground are the balustrade of the light-well which serves the great vaulted basement, and John Bacon's statue of an idealised George III and Father Thames. Behind rises the central feature of Chambers's architectural composition, the dome in the centre of the river range.

Somerset House: West range of the courtyard, view into area
The sculpture here was an afterthought, projecting vulnerably from its niche. All three courtyard ranges stand on double basements, lit from 14 ft [4.2 m] wide areas. Walkways at two levels carried on arches create what has often been called a Piranesian effect. But it is doubtful if Chambers meant these spaces to be appreciated aesthetically, for their walls are roughly scored, not given the careful tooling of stonework elsewhere.

The Interiors

The Royal Academy's premises occupy the western half of the Strand block. The entrance hall is a Doric room, with a swagged frieze derived, says Baretti, 'from a Fragment mentioned in De Cambray's *Parallèle*', and so giving a suitably antique connotation to a space which was dominated by plaster casts of antique statues (see right). The casts of the Furietti *Centaurs* which flank the foot of the stairs were installed early in 1780. To the right was the 'living academy', where the students practised life drawing, a large but plain room (now the Bookshop). At the far end of the hall stands 'an airy screen of fluted Dorick Columns' which 'exhibits a piece of scenery exceedingly agreeable', the stair in its semicircular well rising up and out of sight, the intricate ironwork of its blue-painted balusters silhouetted against the wall (originally stone-coloured).

From the foot of the stair is a view down to the façade of the basement apartment of the Keeper (see following page). This is rusticated and detached from the wall of the stairwell like a stage set. Not surprisingly, the Keeper disliked living underground, and in 1797 the stairwell was floored over and a colossal cast of the Farnese Hercules set up in it. Only in the 1960s was the Keeper's house-front rediscovered.

The staircase is top lit within a slightly cramped semicircular well. Chambers would almost certainly have preferred a circular stairwell but this was one of the compromises which the narrow Strand frontage enforced. Therefore, to quote Baretti again, 'As the Exhibition-Rooms are necessarily, for the light, at the very top of this Stair, the Architect felt the necessity of supplying amusement to the Spectators while mounting towards the sky, and of furnishing them with stations of repose, where they might find entertainment, to compensate for the labour past, and be encouraged to proceed ... every flight of stairs affords a new piece of scenery replete with amusing objects of

Somerset House: Entrance hall, Royal Academy side
Doric is naturally the order used in this ground-level room of entrance. The frieze of lion-heads and swags is imitated from an antique fragment at the Villa Medici, Rome. The plaster-casts of the Furietti centaurs, first set up in 1780, have recently been replaced. The bottom flight of steps with straight baluster-rods cannot be original.

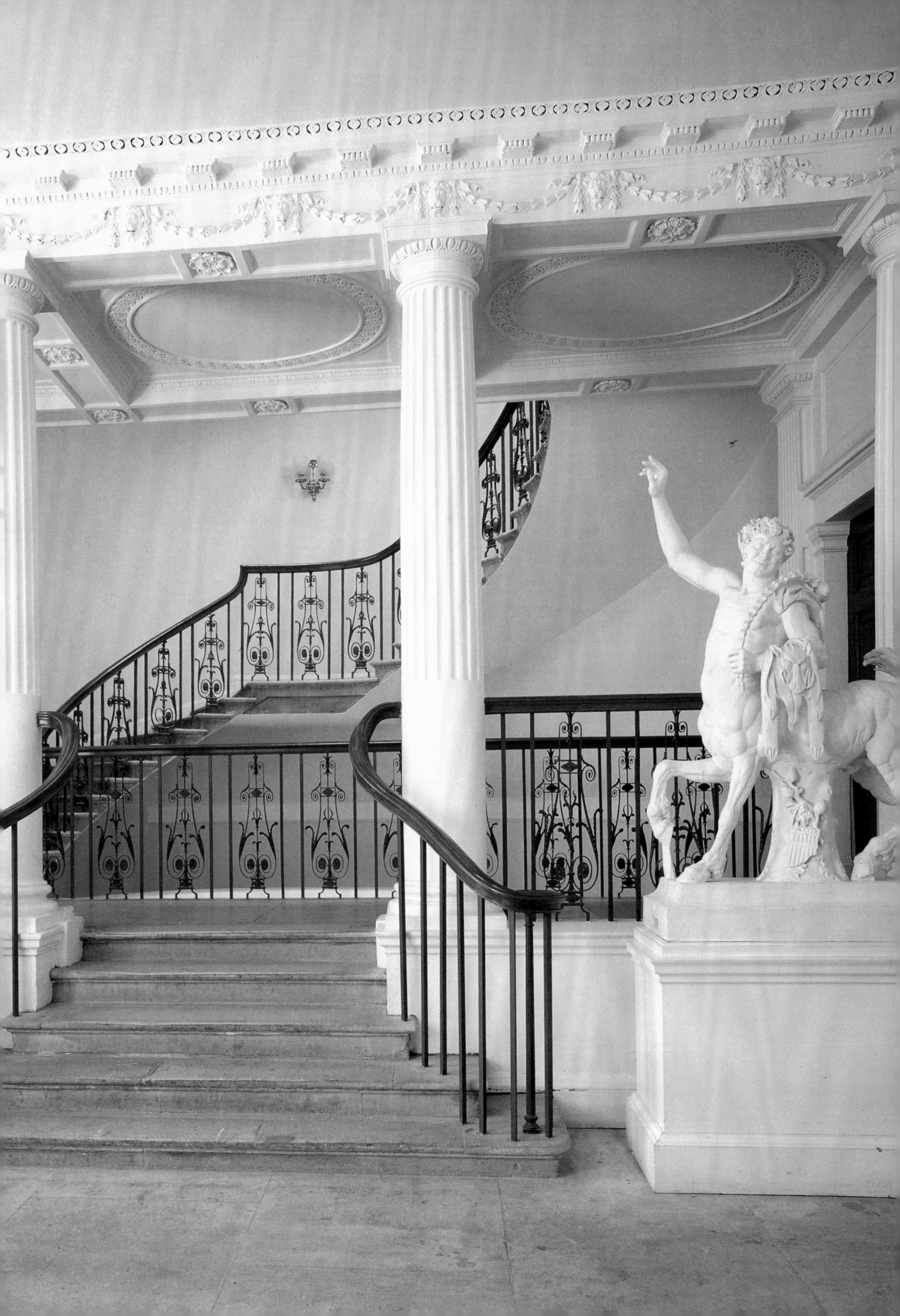

Somerset House: Façade of the Royal
Academy Keeper's house
This unexpected apparition at the foot of the
Royal Academy stair serves to mask the lower
flight of a service staircase. The Keeper soon
refused to live in the basement, and a floor
inserted in 1797 hid his façade until its
rediscovery in the 1960s.

Somerset House: Royal Academy staircase,
detail of balustrade
The elaborate pattern of baluster-panels
delicately echoes the decorative railings of the
Strand front, one of the subtle ways in which
Chambers stressed the Royal Academy's
premises at the expense of those of the other
Societies. The smith was William Palmer.

various sorts.' The first such object, on the landing at
mezzanine level, was a grisaille painting by Cipriani
of putti engaged in painting, sculpture, architecture,
geometry, mathematics and poetry round a bust of
Minerva. Unfortunately this has disappeared, as have
the casts of antique busts of Julius Caesar and
Caligula which flanked it. On this landing the door-
cases are treated with Ionic pilasters.

The next level is the principal floor, where a grand
pedimented doorway of the Composite order (see
right) leads into the first of the Royal Academy's fine
rooms, the square Library (Gallery 6). This hardly
gives the impression of a room devoted to study, in
fact it is difficult to envisage where the bookcases
could have stood. Its central embellishment was Reynolds's ceiling painting (now replaced by a copy)
representing the *Theory of Painting*. In the ceiling cove
there remain Cipriani's brightly coloured paintings
of *Nature*, *History*, *Allegory* and *Fable*, 'the sources
from which the chizzel and pencil gather subjects for

Somerset House: Royal Academy staircase
The architectural effect of the staircase at the principal floor level is particularly splendid. The great height of this storey provides space to insert a coffered arch on which to carry the top landing. The pedimented doorcase, of the Composite order, marks the entrance to the Royal Academy's library and meeting room.

epresentation'. Collins's plasterwork consists of foli-ge pilaster strips on the walls, and in the coves prackets and delicate overlapping swags made up on wires. These ornaments were originally painted white on a purple ground, and there was a good deal of gilding: visitors were clearly meant to be dazzled. The Royal Academy also had two large north-facing rooms at this level, the Antique Academy (Gallery (), its apsidal west end occupied by a large stove (see page 35), and a second show room, the Meeting Room (Gallery 2). The ceiling here was even more spectacular and its present appearance, though still in a way impressive, is a shadow of its former glory. In the centre were five paintings by Benjamin West, a roundel representing the *Graces unveiling Nature*, sur-ounded by a radial arrangement of canvases depicting the *Four Elements*. To set these off Cham-bers designed and Collins executed exotic and memorable plasterwork. The elements of the compo-sition, arabesque foliage, seated lions and winged

maidens, were developed from fragments in the Villa Medici in Rome (the Academy possessed casts); but Baretti rightly stresses how they have been put together so that 'one principle runs through the whole Design, of which the parts seem naturally to rise out of each other'. Set in at the two ends of the ceiling were four oval paintings by Angelica Kauffmann symbolizing Invention, Composition, Design and Colouring. Sadly, when the Royal Academy left Somerset House the paintings went too, and today can be seen in the vestibule ceiling at Burlington House in Piccadilly. Their brilliant colours must have dominated the room originally, though the plas-terwork, now painted a flat white, is described as having been painted with 'shadows' to give relief. Mouldings and foliage were partly gilt and the ground of the ceiling was green and dove grey. All this was apparently not thought to pose a threat to the paintings of the Royal Academicians below, for which frames were fixed to the walls when the room was fitted up.

These were all private rooms. The public face of the Royal Academy was shown at the summer exhibitions for which the Great Room was devised at the top of the building. To reach this it is necessary to mount the third flight of the staircase. Since this has to rise through the full height of the principal storey, it is significantly steeper than the lower two – an unavoidable blemish in the architecture which Rowlandson pilloried in his engraving 'The Stare Case' (see right, above). All the 'amusements' which Chambers could devise are needed here, so the arch which bears the top landing is coffered and its outer face enriched with plasterwork, and opposite there was another even larger painting by Cipriani, now lost. At the top a screen of columns opens into the Anti-Exhibition Room (Gallery 7); they are Corinthian, so here too the visitor experiences the Orders in their proper Chambersian sequence.

For this room J.F. Rigaud executed emblematic paintings; above the doorway to the Great Room (Gallery 8) an inscription (in bad Greek) warns that 'No one uninspired by the Muses may enter'. The Great Room itself 53 ft [16 m] by 43 ft [13 m] by 32 ft [10 m] high, top-lit from four great segmental windows, is sparingly decorated, for it was intended to display paintings hung frame to frame from the floor to the sills of the windows (see right). Charles Catton painted sky and clouds in the central oval of the ceiling and in the angles below groups of putti engaged in painting, sculpture, architecture and geometry.

The eastern half of the Strand block was laid out as a mirror image of the Royal Academy's premises. But it could not be used as such, for here not one but two societies had to be accommodated. Both were under royal patronage, but it is clear that the Royal Society were allocated space first and the Society of Antiquaries established their right to join them as late as January 1776, when Chambers had been working intensively on his design for nearly three months. All the architect could do was to make the two societies share the entrance hall and staircase and an ante-room

E.F. Burney: *The Antique Academy at Somerset House* (Royal Academy of Arts) (*left*)
Drawing from casts after antique statues, as shown in this watercolour of *c*1785, was an important student activity. Prominent statues are (far left) the *'Cincinnatus'*, with, behind, the *Apollo* Belvedere and (far right) the Belvedere *Antinous* and the *Mercury*. The stove was designed by Chambers and supplied by William Bent, ironmonger, for £15 in 1781.

Thomas Rowlandson: *Exhibition Stare Case* (Arthur Ackermann & Son Ltd.) (*right*)
In this coloured aquatint of *c*1811, Rowlandson satirized the inelegant steepness of the top flight of the staircase leading up to the Royal Academy Exhibition Room. Note the representation of Cipriani's 20 ft [6.1 m] long painting which originally faced the top landing. The niche with a statue of Callipygian Venus (Venus of the lovely buttocks) is a piece of artistic licence.

P. Martini after J.H. Ramberg: *The Royal Academy's Great Exhibition Room* (Victoria and Albert Museum) (*below*)
This engraving of 1787 was published to commemorate the visit of the Prince of Wales to the Royal Academy's summer exhibition that year, and shows the Great Room as it was intended to be hung. The way the paintings were hung in relation to the 'line', 7 ft $1\frac{1}{2}$ inches [2.2 m] above floor level, is clearly visible.

on the principal floor. That left a large meeting room for each society at this level in the Strand block. The Antiquaries were allocated a library on the ground floor; the Royal Society had to be content with having both their council room and library in the east wing, the latter at garret level (now Kenneth Clark Memorial lecture room).

As far as possible Chambers fitted up the shared apartments to match those of the Royal Academy, but with certain subtle simplifications: in the Hall the frieze is plain not swagged, and the staircase balustrade is of standard S-scrolls (see right, below). The Ante-room (Gallery 4) is as richly decorated as the R.A. Library, which is its counterpart; but here the inset paintings by Cipriani are monochrome, an *Apollo* head in the centre surrounded by the signs of the zodiac, and in the cove the Four Elements (see far right), all referring to the interests of the Royal Society rather than of the Antiquaries. Heads of philosophers selected by the Secretary of the Royal Society were to occupy the 24 medallions in the wall pilasters. Here the ornaments were painted white on a pink ground, with grey and pink in the ceiling and green in the cove.

The Royal Society's Meeting Room (Gallery 5) is the most monumentally treated of the rooms. Thomas Collins's ceiling has coffering round a large central oval, which may have been intended for a painting but has never been filled. Here the original colour scheme has recently been reinstated on the basis of documentary evidence and paint sampling: green walls and white mouldings set off against pink, green and light purple (see right, above). The heady effect of this must have been considerably subdued by the stout dark furniture, supplied by George Seddon and bolted to the floor, and the serried rows of portraits on the walls (see following page). The Meeting Room of the Society of Antiquaries (Gallery 3) is altogether less spectacular, though originally painted in pink and green to offset the white moulded plasterwork.

The offices which occupied the rest of Somerset House naturally offered much less opportunity for dramatic display. Chambers concentrated on just two. In the centre of the river front was the Seamen's Hall (see following page), which served as the entrance hall to the Navy Office and gave access from the courtyard to the river terrace. Chambers made

Somerset House: Ceiling of the Royal Society's Meeting Room (Gallery 5), detail (*left, above*)
Chambers took great trouble over designing the rose patterns in the coffers and the guilloche band on the dividing beams. The present colour scheme recreates the original: white plasterwork set off against pea green, pink and 'laylock' or light purple. The medallion portrait of George III is answered by one of Charles II, the Society's founder. Thomas Collins was the plasterer.

Somerset House: Royal Society and Society of Antiquaries staircase (*left, below*)
A view up the stairwell shows the semicircular plan and the three flights of stairs. The original ironwork of the skylight is unfortunately lost. The balustrade is of standard S-scrolls. The ironwork was originally painted blue, the walls stone-colour. This is now the main staircase for the Courtauld Institute.

Somerset House: the Ante-room shared by the Royal Society and the Society of Antiquaries (Gallery 4)
This room matches the Royal Academy Library (Gallery 6). The grisaille paintings by G.B. Cipriani in the ceiling represent Apollo (the Sun) surrounded by the signs of the zodiac, and in the cove the Four Elements. The plasterwork is by Thomas Clark. The medallions in the wall pilasters were intended to be filled with heads of philosophers.

Somerset House: Seamen's Hall
In the centre of the river range. This room gave access to the river terrace and was also the entrance hall for the Navy Office. Its correct Doric order, with unfluted scagliola columns and straightforward triglyph and metope frieze, looks like uniform compared with the finery of the apartments in the Strand block.

Anonymous: Royal Society Meeting Room (Royal Society)
This aquatint of c1850 shows the room not long before the Royal Society vacated it, still largely in its original condition. The furniture was supplied by George Seddon in 1780. Note the portraits lining the walls. The chandelier hides the bust of the Society's founder, Charles II, ordered from the sculptor Joseph Nollekens in 1779.

many designs for it, toying with circular and oval plans, but in the end he settled for a deep rectangle, with screens of Doric columns at each end. From this a spine corridor leads to the most exciting space in the whole building, the top-lit oval Navy Staircase (see right) which rises through three storeys, by means of a double flight, a straight flying flight and a long single flight curling round the top of the well. (Within the present Inland Revenue offices, the staircase is not visible to the public.)

Somerset House has on the whole survived with gratifyingly little alteration. The primary reason for this is the fact that it remains in use for its original purpose, as government offices. Today the main courtyard ranges are occupied by the Principal Registry of the Family Division of the High Court (south) and departments of the Inland Revenue (west and east). The learned societies admittedly moved out in the mid-nineteenth century, the Royal Academy in 1837, the others in the mid-1870s. Thereafter the Registrar-General took over their premises, and remained in them until c1970. After remaining empty for nearly twenty years they reopened in 1990 as the Courtauld Institute Galleries. The Courtauld Institute itself, a teaching institution within the University of London devoted to the study of the history of art, has since 1989 occupied the wings of the Strand block, and the great subterranean vaults now house the Institute's libraries of books and photographs.

Somerset House: Navy Staircase
Set in a top-lit oval well, the staircase principally served to lead up to the board-room of the Navy Office. Chambers originally intended to construct two such staircases, at the junctions of the east and west courtyard ranges with the river range, but the eastern one was sacrificed to economy.

Somerset House: Strand block and vaults, north-south section
This recent drawing by Green Lloyd Architects, who designed the conversion for the Courtauld Institute, shows the position of the vaults intended by Chambers for the National Records and now occupied by the Institute's libraries.

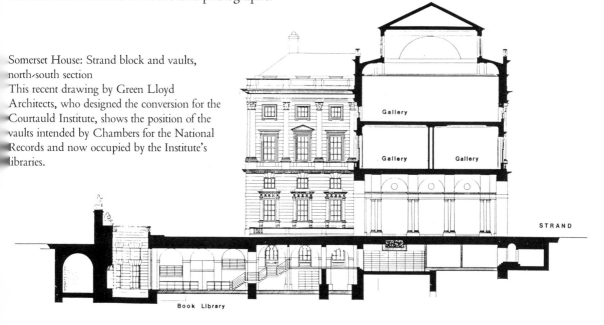

Jean-Louis Desprez: *Idealised view of Somerset House, St Paul's Cathedral and Blackfriars Bridge* (Yale Center for British Art, Paul Mellon collection)

This magnificent watercolour, one of three views of Somerset House by the brilliant French topographical draughtsman J.-L. Desprez included in a sale of Chambers's prints and drawings in 1811, was presumably commissioned by the architect. In most respects the river front is accurately shown, but the redesigned central attic and enlarged dome are incompatible with the executed building. Do they indicate Chambers's dissatisfaction with what he had built?

Edward Dayes: *Somerset House from the river* (Courtauld Institute Galleries)

The original relationship of the embankment and terrace to the river was much more dramatic than it is today. At first Chambers constructed only the central 438 ft [133.5 m] of the river front. Dayes's watercolour of about 1790 shows this before the western end of the composition was completed in 1801.

Sources

Sir William Chambers's correspondence is divided between the British Architectural Library, the library of the Royal Academy and his letter books in the British Library. One key letter is in Sheffield City Archives (WWM Bk 1/802). Of his architectural drawings for Somerset House the great bulk is in the Soane Museum, though one or two important ones are in the Victoria and Albert Museum. Chambers's Parisian drawings are in the RIBA Drawings Collection. The detailed building accounts for Somerset House survive in the British Architectural Library.

Various reports and estimates are published in the *Commons Journals*. Joseph Baretti, *A Guide through the Royal Academy* (1781), is a mine of information. Two authoritative modern publications which draw on these and other materials are John Harris, *Sir William Chambers, Knight of the Polar Star* (London, 1970) and H.M. Colvin, editor, *The History of the King's Works Volume V, 1660–1782* (London, 1976).